Have the most amazing holiday! Can
to hear all abo
in September.   Mrs Kelly x

THIS NOTEBOOK
BELONGS TO:

DATE: S   M   T   W   TH   F   S   ___ ___ ___

PLACE

RATING

☆ ☆ ☆ ☆ ☆

WEATHER

WHAT I DID TODAY

WHAT WAS THE BEST PART ABOUT YOUR DAY?

DRAW OR WRITE ABOUT IT!

I FEEL:

DATE: S   M   T   W   TH   F   S   ___ ___ ___

PLACE

RATING
☆ ☆ ☆ ☆ ☆

WEATHER

WHAT I DID TODAY

WHAT WAS THE BEST PART ABOUT YOUR DAY?

DRAW OR WRITE ABOUT IT!

I FEEL:

DATE: S   M   T   W   TH   F   S   _____ _____ _____

PLACE

_____

RATING _____   ____ WEATHER ____

☆ ☆ ☆ ☆ ☆

_____

WHAT I DID TODAY

_____

_____

_____

_____

WHAT WAS THE BEST PART ABOUT YOUR DAY?

─── DRAW OR WRITE ABOUT IT! ───

I FEEL:

DATE: S   M   T   W   TH   F   S   _____ _____ _____

PLACE

RATING
☆ ☆ ☆ ☆ ☆

WEATHER

WHAT I DID TODAY

WHAT WAS THE BEST PART ABOUT YOUR DAY?
DRAW OR WRITE ABOUT IT!

I FEEL:

DATE: S   M   T   W   TH   F   S   ___ ___ ___

PLACE

RATING

☆ ☆ ☆ ☆ ☆

WEATHER

WHAT I DID TODAY

WHAT WAS THE BEST PART ABOUT YOUR DAY?

DRAW OR WRITE ABOUT IT!

I FEEL:

DATE: S   M   T   W   TH   F   S   ___ ___ ___

PLACE

RATING

☆ ☆ ☆ ☆ ☆

WEATHER

WHAT I DID TODAY

WHAT WAS THE BEST PART ABOUT YOUR DAY?
DRAW OR WRITE ABOUT IT!

I FEEL:

DATE: S   M   T   W   TH   F   S   ⎯⎯ ⎯⎯ ⎯⎯

PLACE

RATING
☆ ☆ ☆ ☆ ☆

WEATHER

WHAT I DID TODAY

WHAT WAS THE BEST PART ABOUT YOUR DAY?
DRAW OR WRITE ABOUT IT!

I FEEL:

DATE: S   M   T   W   TH   F   S   ___ ___ ___

PLACE

RATING
☆ ☆ ☆ ☆ ☆

WEATHER

WHAT I DID TODAY

WHAT WAS THE BEST PART ABOUT YOUR DAY?
DRAW OR WRITE ABOUT IT!

I FEEL:

DATE: S   M   T   W   TH   F   S   ___ ___ ___

PLACE

RATING
☆ ☆ ☆ ☆ ☆

WEATHER

WHAT I DID TODAY

WHAT WAS THE BEST PART ABOUT YOUR DAY?
DRAW OR WRITE ABOUT IT!

I FEEL:

DATE: S   M   T   W   TH   F   S   _____ _____ _____

PLACE

RATING
☆ ☆ ☆ ☆ ☆

WEATHER

WHAT I DID TODAY

WHAT WAS THE BEST PART ABOUT YOUR DAY?
DRAW OR WRITE ABOUT IT!

I FEEL:

DATE: S   M   T   W   TH   F   S   _____ _____ _____

PLACE

RATING
☆ ☆ ☆ ☆ ☆

WEATHER

WHAT I DID TODAY

WHAT WAS THE BEST PART ABOUT YOUR DAY?
DRAW OR WRITE ABOUT IT!

I FEEL:

DATE: S   M   T   W   TH   F   S   ___ ___ ___

PLACE

RATING
☆ ☆ ☆ ☆ ☆

WEATHER

WHAT I DID TODAY

WHAT WAS THE BEST PART ABOUT YOUR DAY?

DRAW OR WRITE ABOUT IT!

I FEEL:

DATE: S   M   T   W   TH   F   S   ___ ___ ___

PLACE

RATING
☆ ☆ ☆ ☆ ☆

WEATHER

WHAT I DID TODAY

WHAT WAS THE BEST PART ABOUT YOUR DAY?
DRAW OR WRITE ABOUT IT!

I FEEL:

DATE: S   M   T   W   TH   F   S   ___ ___ ___

PLACE

RATING
☆ ☆ ☆ ☆ ☆

WEATHER

WHAT I DID TODAY

WHAT WAS THE BEST PART ABOUT YOUR DAY?
DRAW OR WRITE ABOUT IT!

I FEEL:

DATE: S   M   T   W   TH   F   S   ___ ___ ___

PLACE

RATING
☆ ☆ ☆ ☆ ☆

WEATHER

WHAT I DID TODAY

WHAT WAS THE BEST PART ABOUT YOUR DAY?
DRAW OR WRITE ABOUT IT!

I FEEL:

DATE: S   M   T   W   TH   F   S   ____ ____ ____

PLACE

RATING

☆ ☆ ☆ ☆ ☆

WEATHER

WHAT I DID TODAY

WHAT WAS THE BEST PART ABOUT YOUR DAY?

DRAW OR WRITE ABOUT IT!

I FEEL:

DATE: S   M   T   W   TH   F   S   ____ ____ ____

PLACE

RATING
☆ ☆ ☆ ☆ ☆

WEATHER

WHAT I DID TODAY

WHAT WAS THE BEST PART ABOUT YOUR DAY?
DRAW OR WRITE ABOUT IT!

I FEEL:

DATE: S M T W TH F S ____ ____ ____

PLACE

RATING
☆ ☆ ☆ ☆ ☆

WEATHER

WHAT I DID TODAY

WHAT WAS THE BEST PART ABOUT YOUR DAY?
DRAW OR WRITE ABOUT IT!

I FEEL:

DATE: S   M   T   W   TH   F   S   ___ ___ ___

PLACE

RATING

☆ ☆ ☆ ☆ ☆

WEATHER

WHAT I DID TODAY

WHAT WAS THE BEST PART ABOUT YOUR DAY?
DRAW OR WRITE ABOUT IT!

I FEEL:

DATE: S   M   T   W   TH   F   S   ___ ___ ___

PLACE

RATING
☆ ☆ ☆ ☆ ☆

WEATHER

WHAT I DID TODAY

WHAT WAS THE BEST PART ABOUT YOUR DAY?
DRAW OR WRITE ABOUT IT!

I FEEL:

DATE: S   M   T   W   TH   F   S   ___ ___ ___

PLACE

_____

RATING
☆ ☆ ☆ ☆ ☆

WEATHER
_____

WHAT I DID TODAY
_____
_____
_____
_____

WHAT WAS THE BEST PART ABOUT YOUR DAY?
DRAW OR WRITE ABOUT IT!

I FEEL:

DATE: S   M   T   W   TH   F   S   —— —— ——

PLACE

RATING

☆ ☆ ☆ ☆ ☆

WEATHER

WHAT I DID TODAY

WHAT WAS THE BEST PART ABOUT YOUR DAY?

DRAW OR WRITE ABOUT IT!

I FEEL:

DATE: S   M   T   W   TH   F   S   ___ ___ ___

PLACE

RATING

☆ ☆ ☆ ☆ ☆

WEATHER

WHAT I DID TODAY

WHAT WAS THE BEST PART ABOUT YOUR DAY?

DRAW OR WRITE ABOUT IT!

I FEEL:

DATE: S M T W TH F S ___ ___ ___

PLACE

RATING

☆ ☆ ☆ ☆ ☆

WEATHER

WHAT I DID TODAY

WHAT WAS THE BEST PART ABOUT YOUR DAY?
DRAW OR WRITE ABOUT IT!

I FEEL:

DATE: S   M   T   W   TH   F   S   ___ ___ ___

PLACE

RATING
☆ ☆ ☆ ☆ ☆

WEATHER

WHAT I DID TODAY

WHAT WAS THE BEST PART ABOUT YOUR DAY?
DRAW OR WRITE ABOUT IT!

I FEEL:

DATE: S M T W TH F S ___ ___ ___

PLACE

RATING
☆ ☆ ☆ ☆ ☆

WEATHER

WHAT I DID TODAY

WHAT WAS THE BEST PART ABOUT YOUR DAY?
DRAW OR WRITE ABOUT IT!

I FEEL:

DATE: S   M   T   W   TH   F   S   ___ ___ ___

PLACE

RATING
☆ ☆ ☆ ☆ ☆

WEATHER

WHAT I DID TODAY

WHAT WAS THE BEST PART ABOUT YOUR DAY?
DRAW OR WRITE ABOUT IT!

I FEEL:

DATE: S   M   T   W   TH   F   S   ____ ____ ____

PLACE

RATING
☆ ☆ ☆ ☆ ☆

WEATHER

WHAT I DID TODAY

WHAT WAS THE BEST PART ABOUT YOUR DAY?

DRAW OR WRITE ABOUT IT!

I FEEL:

DATE: S   M   T   W   TH   F   S   _____ _____ _____

PLACE

RATING
☆ ☆ ☆ ☆ ☆

WEATHER

WHAT I DID TODAY

WHAT WAS THE BEST PART ABOUT YOUR DAY?
DRAW OR WRITE ABOUT IT!

I FEEL:

DATE: S   M   T   W   TH   F   S   ___ ___ ___

PLACE

RATING

☆ ☆ ☆ ☆ ☆

WEATHER

WHAT I DID TODAY

WHAT WAS THE BEST PART ABOUT YOUR DAY?
DRAW OR WRITE ABOUT IT!

I FEEL:

DATE: S M T W TH F S ___ ___ ___

PLACE

RATING
☆ ☆ ☆ ☆ ☆

WEATHER

WHAT I DID TODAY

WHAT WAS THE BEST PART ABOUT YOUR DAY?
DRAW OR WRITE ABOUT IT!

I FEEL:

DATE: S   M   T   W   TH   F   S   ___ ___ ___

PLACE

RATING
☆ ☆ ☆ ☆ ☆

WEATHER

WHAT I DID TODAY

WHAT WAS THE BEST PART ABOUT YOUR DAY?

DRAW OR WRITE ABOUT IT!

I FEEL:

DATE: S M T W TH F S _____ _____ _____

PLACE

RATING
☆ ☆ ☆ ☆ ☆

WEATHER

WHAT I DID TODAY

WHAT WAS THE BEST PART ABOUT YOUR DAY?
DRAW OR WRITE ABOUT IT!

I FEEL:

DATE: S   M   T   W   TH   F   S   _____ _____ _____

PLACE

RATING
☆ ☆ ☆ ☆ ☆

WEATHER

WHAT I DID TODAY

WHAT WAS THE BEST PART ABOUT YOUR DAY?
DRAW OR WRITE ABOUT IT!

I FEEL:

DATE: S   M   T   W   TH   F   S   _____ _____ _____

PLACE

RATING
☆ ☆ ☆ ☆ ☆

WEATHER

WHAT I DID TODAY

WHAT WAS THE BEST PART ABOUT YOUR DAY?
DRAW OR WRITE ABOUT IT!

I FEEL:

DATE: S   M   T   W   TH   F   S   ___ ___ ___

PLACE

RATING
☆ ☆ ☆ ☆ ☆

WEATHER

WHAT I DID TODAY

WHAT WAS THE BEST PART ABOUT YOUR DAY?
DRAW OR WRITE ABOUT IT!

I FEEL:

DATE: S M T W TH F S ___ ___ ___

PLACE

RATING
☆ ☆ ☆ ☆ ☆

WEATHER

WHAT I DID TODAY

WHAT WAS THE BEST PART ABOUT YOUR DAY?
DRAW OR WRITE ABOUT IT!

I FEEL:

DATE: S   M   T   W   TH   F   S   _____ _____ _____

PLACE

RATING
☆ ☆ ☆ ☆ ☆

WEATHER

WHAT I DID TODAY

WHAT WAS THE BEST PART ABOUT YOUR DAY?
DRAW OR WRITE ABOUT IT!

I FEEL:

DATE: S   M   T   W   TH   F   S   ___ ___ ___

PLACE

RATING
☆ ☆ ☆ ☆ ☆

WEATHER

WHAT I DID TODAY

WHAT WAS THE BEST PART ABOUT YOUR DAY?
DRAW OR WRITE ABOUT IT!

I FEEL:

DATE: S   M   T   W   TH   F   S   ____ ____ ____

PLACE

RATING
☆ ☆ ☆ ☆ ☆

WEATHER

WHAT I DID TODAY

WHAT WAS THE BEST PART ABOUT YOUR DAY?
DRAW OR WRITE ABOUT IT!

I FEEL:

DATE: S   M   T   W   TH   F   S   ___ ___ ___

PLACE

RATING
☆ ☆ ☆ ☆ ☆

WEATHER

WHAT I DID TODAY

WHAT WAS THE BEST PART ABOUT YOUR DAY?
DRAW OR WRITE ABOUT IT!

I FEEL:

DATE: S   M   T   W   TH   F   S   _____ _____ _____

PLACE

_____

RATING _____   _____ WEATHER

☆ ☆ ☆ ☆ ☆ | _____

WHAT I DID TODAY

_____

_____

_____

_____

WHAT WAS THE BEST PART ABOUT YOUR DAY?

DRAW OR WRITE ABOUT IT!

I FEEL:

DATE: S M T W TH F S ___ ___ ___

PLACE

RATING

☆ ☆ ☆ ☆ ☆

WEATHER

WHAT I DID TODAY

WHAT WAS THE BEST PART ABOUT YOUR DAY?

DRAW OR WRITE ABOUT IT!

I FEEL:

DATE: S   M   T   W   TH   F   S   ____ ____ ____

PLACE

RATING

☆ ☆ ☆ ☆ ☆

WEATHER

WHAT I DID TODAY

WHAT WAS THE BEST PART ABOUT YOUR DAY?
DRAW OR WRITE ABOUT IT!

I FEEL:

DATE: S   M   T   W   TH   F   S   _____ _____ _____

PLACE

_____

RATING

☆ ☆ ☆ ☆ ☆

WEATHER

_____

WHAT I DID TODAY

_____

_____

_____

_____

I FEEL:

WHAT WAS THE BEST PART ABOUT YOUR DAY?
DRAW OR WRITE ABOUT IT!

DATE: S   M   T   W   TH   F   S   _____ _____ _____

PLACE

RATING

☆ ☆ ☆ ☆ ☆

WEATHER

WHAT I DID TODAY

WHAT WAS THE BEST PART ABOUT YOUR DAY?
DRAW OR WRITE ABOUT IT!

I FEEL:

DATE: S   M   T   W   TH   F   S   ⎯⎯ ⎯⎯ ⎯⎯

PLACE

RATING

☆ ☆ ☆ ☆ ☆

WEATHER

WHAT I DID TODAY

WHAT WAS THE BEST PART ABOUT YOUR DAY?
DRAW OR WRITE ABOUT IT!

I FEEL:

DATE: S   M   T   W   TH   F   S   ___ ___ ___

PLACE

RATING
☆ ☆ ☆ ☆ ☆

WEATHER

WHAT I DID TODAY

WHAT WAS THE BEST PART ABOUT YOUR DAY?

DRAW OR WRITE ABOUT IT!

I FEEL:

DATE: S   M   T   W   TH   F   S   ___ ___ ___

PLACE

RATING
☆ ☆ ☆ ☆ ☆

WEATHER

WHAT I DID TODAY

WHAT WAS THE BEST PART ABOUT YOUR DAY?
DRAW OR WRITE ABOUT IT!

I FEEL:

DATE: S   M   T   W   TH   F   S   ___ ___ ___

PLACE

RATING
☆ ☆ ☆ ☆ ☆

WEATHER

WHAT I DID TODAY

WHAT WAS THE BEST PART ABOUT YOUR DAY?
DRAW OR WRITE ABOUT IT!

I FEEL:

DATE: S   M   T   W   TH   F   S   _____ __ __

PLACE

RATING
☆ ☆ ☆ ☆ ☆

WEATHER

WHAT I DID TODAY

WHAT WAS THE BEST PART ABOUT YOUR DAY?
DRAW OR WRITE ABOUT IT!

I FEEL:

DATE: S   M   T   W   TH   F   S   _____ _____ _____

PLACE

RATING

☆ ☆ ☆ ☆ ☆

WEATHER

WHAT I DID TODAY

WHAT WAS THE BEST PART ABOUT YOUR DAY?

DRAW OR WRITE ABOUT IT!

I FEEL:

DATE: S   M   T   W   TH   F   S   —— —— ——

PLACE

RATING
☆ ☆ ☆ ☆ ☆

WEATHER

WHAT I DID TODAY

WHAT WAS THE BEST PART ABOUT YOUR DAY?
DRAW OR WRITE ABOUT IT!

I FEEL:

DATE: S   M   T   W   TH   F   S   _____ _____ _____

PLACE

RATING
☆ ☆ ☆ ☆ ☆

WEATHER

WHAT I DID TODAY

WHAT WAS THE BEST PART ABOUT YOUR DAY?
DRAW OR WRITE ABOUT IT!

I FEEL:

DATE: S   M   T   W   TH   F   S   _____ _____ _____

PLACE

RATING
☆ ☆ ☆ ☆ ☆

WEATHER

WHAT I DID TODAY

WHAT WAS THE BEST PART ABOUT YOUR DAY?
DRAW OR WRITE ABOUT IT!

I FEEL:

DATE: S   M   T   W   TH   F   S   ____ ____ ____

PLACE

RATING
☆ ☆ ☆ ☆ ☆

WEATHER

WHAT I DID TODAY

WHAT WAS THE BEST PART ABOUT YOUR DAY?

DRAW OR WRITE ABOUT IT!

I FEEL:

DATE: S   M   T   W   TH   F   S   ___ ___ ___

PLACE

RATING
☆ ☆ ☆ ☆ ☆

WEATHER

WHAT I DID TODAY

WHAT WAS THE BEST PART ABOUT YOUR DAY?
DRAW OR WRITE ABOUT IT!

I FEEL:

DATE: S   M   T   W   TH   F   S   —— — —— —

PLACE

RATING
☆ ☆ ☆ ☆ ☆

WEATHER

WHAT I DID TODAY

WHAT WAS THE BEST PART ABOUT YOUR DAY?
DRAW OR WRITE ABOUT IT!

I FEEL:

DATE: S   M   T   W   TH   F   S   ___ ___ ___

PLACE

RATING
☆ ☆ ☆ ☆ ☆

WEATHER

WHAT I DID TODAY

WHAT WAS THE BEST PART ABOUT YOUR DAY?

DRAW OR WRITE ABOUT IT!

I FEEL:

DATE: S   M   T   W   TH   F   S   _____ _____ _____

PLACE

RATING
☆ ☆ ☆ ☆ ☆

WEATHER

WHAT I DID TODAY

WHAT WAS THE BEST PART ABOUT YOUR DAY?

DRAW OR WRITE ABOUT IT!

I FEEL:

DATE: S   M   T   W   TH   F   S   ____ ____ ____

PLACE

RATING
☆ ☆ ☆ ☆ ☆

WEATHER

WHAT I DID TODAY

WHAT WAS THE BEST PART ABOUT YOUR DAY?
DRAW OR WRITE ABOUT IT!

I FEEL:

DATE: S   M   T   W   TH   F   S   ___ ___ ___

PLACE

RATING
☆ ☆ ☆ ☆ ☆

WEATHER

WHAT I DID TODAY

WHAT WAS THE BEST PART ABOUT YOUR DAY?
DRAW OR WRITE ABOUT IT!

I FEEL:

DATE: S   M   T   W   TH   F   S   ___ ___ ___

PLACE

RATING
☆ ☆ ☆ ☆ ☆

WEATHER

WHAT I DID TODAY

WHAT WAS THE BEST PART ABOUT YOUR DAY?
DRAW OR WRITE ABOUT IT!

I FEEL:

DATE: S   M   T   W   TH   F   S   ____ ____ ____

PLACE

RATING

☆ ☆ ☆ ☆ ☆

WEATHER

WHAT I DID TODAY

WHAT WAS THE BEST PART ABOUT YOUR DAY?
DRAW OR WRITE ABOUT IT!

I FEEL:

DATE: S   M   T   W   TH   F   S   ___ ___ ___

PLACE

RATING
☆ ☆ ☆ ☆ ☆

WEATHER

WHAT I DID TODAY

WHAT WAS THE BEST PART ABOUT YOUR DAY?
DRAW OR WRITE ABOUT IT!

I FEEL:

DATE: S   M   T   W   TH   F   S   ___ ___ ___

PLACE

RATING
☆ ☆ ☆ ☆ ☆

WEATHER

WHAT I DID TODAY

WHAT WAS THE BEST PART ABOUT YOUR DAY?

DRAW OR WRITE ABOUT IT!

I FEEL:

DATE: S M T W TH F S ___ ___ ___

PLACE

RATING
☆ ☆ ☆ ☆ ☆

WEATHER

WHAT I DID TODAY

WHAT WAS THE BEST PART ABOUT YOUR DAY?
DRAW OR WRITE ABOUT IT!

I FEEL:

DATE: S   M   T   W   TH   F   S   ___ ___ ___

PLACE

RATING
☆ ☆ ☆ ☆ ☆

WEATHER

WHAT I DID TODAY

WHAT WAS THE BEST PART ABOUT YOUR DAY?
DRAW OR WRITE ABOUT IT!

I FEEL:

DATE: S   M   T   W   TH   F   S   ___ ___ ___

PLACE

RATING
☆ ☆ ☆ ☆ ☆

WEATHER

WHAT I DID TODAY

WHAT WAS THE BEST PART ABOUT YOUR DAY?
DRAW OR WRITE ABOUT IT!

I FEEL:

DATE: S   M   T   W   TH   F   S   _____ _____ _____

PLACE

RATING
☆ ☆ ☆ ☆ ☆

WEATHER

WHAT I DID TODAY

WHAT WAS THE BEST PART ABOUT YOUR DAY?

DRAW OR WRITE ABOUT IT!

I FEEL:

DATE: S   M   T   W   TH   F   S   ___ ___ ___

PLACE

RATING
☆ ☆ ☆ ☆ ☆

WEATHER

WHAT I DID TODAY

WHAT WAS THE BEST PART ABOUT YOUR DAY?
DRAW OR WRITE ABOUT IT!

I FEEL:

DATE: S   M   T   W   TH   F   S   ___ ___ ___

PLACE

RATING
☆ ☆ ☆ ☆ ☆

WEATHER

WHAT I DID TODAY

WHAT WAS THE BEST PART ABOUT YOUR DAY?

DRAW OR WRITE ABOUT IT!

I FEEL:

DATE: S   M   T   W   TH   F   S   ____ ____ ____

PLACE

RATING
☆ ☆ ☆ ☆ ☆

WEATHER

WHAT I DID TODAY

WHAT WAS THE BEST PART ABOUT YOUR DAY?

DRAW OR WRITE ABOUT IT!

I FEEL:

DATE: S   M   T   W   TH   F   S   ____ ____ ____

PLACE

RATING
☆ ☆ ☆ ☆ ☆

WEATHER

WHAT I DID TODAY

WHAT WAS THE BEST PART ABOUT YOUR DAY?
DRAW OR WRITE ABOUT IT!

I FEEL:

DATE: S   M   T   W   TH   F   S   ___ ___ ___

PLACE

RATING
☆ ☆ ☆ ☆ ☆

WEATHER

WHAT I DID TODAY

WHAT WAS THE BEST PART ABOUT YOUR DAY?
DRAW OR WRITE ABOUT IT!

I FEEL:

DATE: S   M   T   W   TH   F   S   ___ ___ ___

PLACE

RATING
☆ ☆ ☆ ☆ ☆

WEATHER

WHAT I DID TODAY

WHAT WAS THE BEST PART ABOUT YOUR DAY?
DRAW OR WRITE ABOUT IT!

I FEEL:

DATE: S   M   T   W   TH   F   S   ___ ___ ___

PLACE

RATING
☆ ☆ ☆ ☆ ☆

WEATHER

WHAT I DID TODAY

WHAT WAS THE BEST PART ABOUT YOUR DAY?
DRAW OR WRITE ABOUT IT!

I FEEL:

DATE: S   M   T   W   TH   F   S   ____ ____ ____

PLACE

RATING
☆ ☆ ☆ ☆ ☆

WEATHER

WHAT I DID TODAY

WHAT WAS THE BEST PART ABOUT YOUR DAY?
DRAW OR WRITE ABOUT IT!

I FEEL:

DATE: S   M   T   W   TH   F   S   ___ ___ ___

PLACE

RATING
☆ ☆ ☆ ☆ ☆

WEATHER

WHAT I DID TODAY

WHAT WAS THE BEST PART ABOUT YOUR DAY?
DRAW OR WRITE ABOUT IT!

I FEEL:

DATE: S   M   T   W   TH   F   S   ____ ____ __

PLACE

RATING

☆ ☆ ☆ ☆ ☆

WEATHER

WHAT I DID TODAY

WHAT WAS THE BEST PART ABOUT YOUR DAY?

DRAW OR WRITE ABOUT IT!

I FEEL:

DATE: S   M   T   W   TH   F   S   ____ ____ ____

PLACE

RATING

☆ ☆ ☆ ☆ ☆

WEATHER

WHAT I DID TODAY

WHAT WAS THE BEST PART ABOUT YOUR DAY?
DRAW OR WRITE ABOUT IT!

I FEEL:

DATE: S   M   T   W   TH   F   S   ____   ____   ____

PLACE

RATING
☆ ☆ ☆ ☆ ☆

WEATHER

WHAT I DID TODAY

WHAT WAS THE BEST PART ABOUT YOUR DAY?
DRAW OR WRITE ABOUT IT!

I FEEL:

DATE: S   M   T   W   TH   F   S   ____ ____ ____

PLACE

RATING
☆ ☆ ☆ ☆ ☆

WEATHER

WHAT I DID TODAY

WHAT WAS THE BEST PART ABOUT YOUR DAY?
DRAW OR WRITE ABOUT IT!

I FEEL:

DATE: S   M   T   W   TH   F   S   ___ ___ ___

PLACE

RATING
☆ ☆ ☆ ☆ ☆

WEATHER

WHAT I DID TODAY

WHAT WAS THE BEST PART ABOUT YOUR DAY?
DRAW OR WRITE ABOUT IT!

I FEEL:

DATE: S   M   T   W   TH   F   S   _____ _____ _____

PLACE

RATING
☆ ☆ ☆ ☆ ☆

WEATHER

WHAT I DID TODAY

WHAT WAS THE BEST PART ABOUT YOUR DAY?
DRAW OR WRITE ABOUT IT!

I FEEL:

DATE: S   M   T   W   TH   F   S   ___ ___ ___

PLACE

RATING

☆ ☆ ☆ ☆ ☆

WEATHER

WHAT I DID TODAY

WHAT WAS THE BEST PART ABOUT YOUR DAY?

DRAW OR WRITE ABOUT IT!

I FEEL:

DATE: S   M   T   W   TH   F   S   ____ ____ ____

PLACE

RATING
☆ ☆ ☆ ☆ ☆

WEATHER

WHAT I DID TODAY

WHAT WAS THE BEST PART ABOUT YOUR DAY?
DRAW OR WRITE ABOUT IT!

I FEEL:

DATE: S   M   T   W   TH   F   S   ___ ___ ___

PLACE

RATING

☆ ☆ ☆ ☆ ☆

WEATHER

WHAT I DID TODAY

WHAT WAS THE BEST PART ABOUT YOUR DAY?
DRAW OR WRITE ABOUT IT!

I FEEL:

DATE: S   M   T   W   TH   F   S   _____ _____ _____

PLACE

RATING
☆ ☆ ☆ ☆ ☆

WEATHER

WHAT I DID TODAY

WHAT WAS THE BEST PART ABOUT YOUR DAY?
DRAW OR WRITE ABOUT IT!

I FEEL:

DATE: S   M   T   W   TH   F   S   ___ ___ ___

PLACE

RATING
☆ ☆ ☆ ☆ ☆

WEATHER

WHAT I DID TODAY

WHAT WAS THE BEST PART ABOUT YOUR DAY?
DRAW OR WRITE ABOUT IT!

I FEEL:

DATE: S M T W TH F S ___ ___ ___

PLACE

RATING
☆ ☆ ☆ ☆ ☆

WEATHER

WHAT I DID TODAY

WHAT WAS THE BEST PART ABOUT YOUR DAY?
DRAW OR WRITE ABOUT IT!

I FEEL:

DATE: S   M   T   W   TH   F   S   ___ ___ ___

PLACE

RATING
☆ ☆ ☆ ☆ ☆

WEATHER

WHAT I DID TODAY

WHAT WAS THE BEST PART ABOUT YOUR DAY?
DRAW OR WRITE ABOUT IT!

I FEEL:

DATE: S   M   T   W   TH   F   S   ___ ___ ___

PLACE

RATING
☆ ☆ ☆ ☆ ☆

WEATHER

WHAT I DID TODAY

WHAT WAS THE BEST PART ABOUT YOUR DAY?
DRAW OR WRITE ABOUT IT!

I FEEL:

DATE: S   M   T   W   TH   F   S   _____ _____ _____

PLACE

RATING   WEATHER
☆ ☆ ☆ ☆ ☆

WHAT I DID TODAY

WHAT WAS THE BEST PART ABOUT YOUR DAY?
DRAW OR WRITE ABOUT IT!

I FEEL:

DATE: S M T W TH F S ____ ____ ____

PLACE

RATING

☆ ☆ ☆ ☆ ☆

WEATHER

WHAT I DID TODAY

WHAT WAS THE BEST PART ABOUT YOUR DAY?
DRAW OR WRITE ABOUT IT!

I FEEL:

DATE: S   M   T   W   TH   F   S   ___ ___ ___

PLACE

RATING
☆ ☆ ☆ ☆ ☆

WEATHER

WHAT I DID TODAY

WHAT WAS THE BEST PART ABOUT YOUR DAY?
DRAW OR WRITE ABOUT IT!

I FEEL:

DATE: S   M   T   W   TH   F   S   _____ _____ _____

PLACE

RATING
☆ ☆ ☆ ☆ ☆

WEATHER

WHAT I DID TODAY

WHAT WAS THE BEST PART ABOUT YOUR DAY?
DRAW OR WRITE ABOUT IT!

I FEEL:

Printed in Great Britain
by Amazon

78750946R00059